POEMS OF DIVORCE

by

S.M. WINTER

Copyright © 2024 by S.M. Winter.

All rights reserved.

No portion of this book may be reproduced in any form without written permission from the author.

ISBN 978-1-7383172-0-2

for
my grandmother
my mother
and my daughter

thank you
to my husband
for the encouragement
and safe loving space
always

PREFACE

The best description of my insides is that of an over-full garbage can; I keep pushing more trash down and packing it full, yet have nowhere to take the trash to. Maintain composure, take the high road, don't react, let it go. I felt like I had no outlet after my divorce. As much as my support system was crucial all those years, no one could *really* relate. I poured my pain into the notes app on my phone, not thinking much of it other than, it was a good release at the time.

Recently I scrolled through my notes and thought, I should publish this. Someone- maybe even one person on this earth- might understand. There's no way I can be the only one. Hide the pain, stuff it down, put a smile on, move forward. Time has truly been the only healer.

As I copied my thoughts and poems into a document, I felt closure. Seeing the words on printed paper was completing a chapter inside me that needed to be set aside. Almost like all this heartache wasn't for nothing. It was something tangible, I could touch and feel and then tuck away on a bookshelf.

I'm still not sure if I have the confidence to do this. So if you're reading this, just know I overcame all my fears. And if this resonates with you, you have my heart dear friend. You are not alone, I'm right there with you.

All my love,

POEMS OF DIVORCE

contents

INTRO...5
FINDING OUT...6
LIAR..7
TANGO...9
VOWS..10
SINNER..11
MOTHER COMFORT......................................13
HATRED..14
UNSOLVED..15
MASCARA..17
MISTRESS...18
ABORTION...19
SLUMBER...20
BED..21
MYOPIC..23
SCREAM...24
GROUP CHAT..25
SHARED CUSTODY.......................................27
COMBUST..28
GHOSTS..29
LULLABY...31
?...32
25 TO LIFE...33
CARPENTER...35
AFTERSHOCK..36
WAGER...37
BLUE EYES...39
FOCUS..40
FAIRYTALE...41
CLOSURE...42
MEDICATE..43
FREEDOM...44
ADVICE I...45
SPARKLE...46

postscript

GENERATIONS...49
ADVICE II..50
THERAPY..51

POEMS OF DIVORCE

INTRO

If you're reading this,
I overcame all my fears.

FINDING OUT

i lay in our bed
on my side
staring out the window
hard to see
looking through a murky lake
my stomach is an abandoned quarry
my heart, well–
it's noon but i've never seen day
look like the darkest night
i can't move an inch

and if i'm being honest
i can't tell if i'm even alive

LIAR

you claim you never once loved me
but i still remember vividly
every moment you did

TANGO

the only times i've ever considered killing myself
were because of you.

a dance with the devil
in the midnight ballroom
of my skull
you,
or your absence–
the orchestra
keeping our pace

but somewhere between
the tango and waltz
i covered my ears
and broke step

VOWS

It's okay, those vows weren't binding anyway.

SINNER

broken frames
wedding photos
cover our floors

in the trash
the book of love
i wrote to you
your wedding gift

i can't tell if a worse sin
is you leaving
or you disgracing
our love
in our home

MOTHER COMFORT

"It's okay Mommy"
She says as she rubs my back.
-My daughter, 2 years old.

HATRED

I have the most disdain for men like you.

UNSOLVED

To have you condemn my father
for how he treated my mother
then turn and do the same
is a puzzle i'll never solve.

MASCARA

Today it's raining. I dug through my makeup drawer to find waterproof mascara, because even when it's raining, I still want to feel pretty.

As I was applying it, it dawned on me that this is the same tube of mascara I bought for my wedding day. "So exciting," cheered the kind lady who assisted me. I had only used it that day, so I wouldn't have makeup running down my face when I cried tears of joy, marrying the man of my dreams. Then, it sat idle in my makeup drawer, forgotten in the back. Weeks after he left, I reached for that same tube. When I was finally ready to peel my body off the floor and face myself in the mirror. Still unable to get through a day without crumbling. I used it again the day he drove me to the clinic. It kept my eyelashes intact while I tried to hold back an ocean of tears as they ended the sweet, innocent life inside my body.

After that, I stopped caring if makeup ran down my face or not. No judgment from anyone could ever compare to the judgment I kept for myself. But today, I applied that mascara again. Because it's raining outside, and I wanted to feel pretty. Not because I'm worried I will crack under the weight of it all. Just because I want to feel pretty.

The man who swore to love me for better or for worse before God has abandoned me before my mascara tube has even had the chance to run dry.

I laugh until I cry.

MISTRESS

how do you sleep at night?
mother karma
always catches up
i pray—
i would not wish this
on even you
nothing can prepare you—
the heartbreak
my fate could be yours

because he won't love you forever
there will be another you

ABORTION

the innocent victim of our demise
resting in peace
unlike us

was it even a choice

SLUMBER

i close my eyes–
the deeper i breathe
the slower i breathe
the faster my heart beats
spinning loops of dread

i open my eyes–
  light switch
     wall
  dresser
    door

i close my eyes–
breathe
try again
i can do this

BED

you fall to your knees
weeping
it's my fault, you cry
i've ruined your life.

no sir,
you made your bed
now lie in it.

MYOPIC

tossed our promise
forged your secret

hid in shadows
seized your moment

such brute force
prognosis unknown

failing to notice
the audience

small set of eyes
witnessing mommy break

SCREAM

your words of hatred
spew tirelessly
trying to soak me
'til i drown

but do you see?
come closer
i'm not angry
i'm not yelling back
i can see you
it's okay to
        project
one day you will see
until then
keep yelling at me
louder this time
LOUDER
do you hear it yet?

listen–
i'll wait 'til you're ready

GROUP CHAT

hide behind your screen
send your dirty letters
they used to make me spiral
i'll never share your words

but just so you know
my family group chat is lit

SHARED CUSTODY

Always in my heart
I tell her, where I keep her
Always in your heart
I tell her, where she can keep me

COMBUST

you can't even look at me
maybe you'll combust
if your eyes meet mine

GHOSTS

out the corner of my eye
i see
the haunting ghosts
of your crimes
stalking me
permanent shadows
fixtures i've grown accustomed to

i shut my eyes
warm rays of sun
thaw my weary lids—
a brief moment of bliss
before the cool breeze
caresses up my spine
taunting me

i'm never alone anymore

LULLABY

I stroke your hair,
You're unaware—
This is my only happy place.
Singing softly to you,
My sunshine, my moon.
I can breathe you in,
Safe at home,
In my arms.
Singing softly to you,
You are my sunshine
My only sunshine
A depth in those words,
Maybe it's heard,
As my voice cracks
On *happy*.
You may never know *dear*,
How deep this goes,
Treasuring every moment
With you.

?

I screamed it over and over
knowingly into the abyss
until my throat was hoarse
cracked and dry–

why

25 TO LIFE

you must be miserable
stuck in the prison you made
that's why you try to
drag me down
meet in your cold cage
rotting, sinking, reaching

as much as i should
leave you trapped
i'd find the keys if you asked
try each one until the lock clicked
open

CARPENTER

the door shut
thunder echoed the space
this empty house
you drove away
left nothing
but this hollow shell
come back

time passed

i filled the space
fashioned my
racing thoughts
into couches
tears into a bed
come back

it wasn't 'til
each room was
furnished
that i realized–
you never heard me

AFTERSHOCK

you ripped life from me
i still bleed sometimes

WAGER

perhaps you are well
perhaps you are thriving
perhaps you bet your dollar
on a tarnished silver lining

BLUE EYES

i don't envy the day she grows up
and realizes
we all had that day–
when we discovered our parents
were just people

but i don't envy that day for you
i've protected you all these years
but i can't protect you from that
i'm at peace for the moment she discovers me
i have no shame
i don't envy that day
she'll see right through you

she has my eyes

FOCUS

You are the greatest mom for her
Your final kind words to me
They are etched in my psyche
I hang on for dear life
I didn't sign up for this ride of terror
I tune into that moment
Try to drown out the madness

FAIRYTALE

i can't seem to forgive you
for making our child only know
a broken home
she was too young to remember
the love we shared
i tell her stories of a life
she won't recall

shame on you for making them fairy tales

CLOSURE

i'm curious,
can a lack of closure kill you?

i guess i'll let you know.

MEDICATE

for a few years
self-induced coma;
memory washed into fog..
but now I am
present
my heart and soul needed a rest

sad sleeping beauty

FREEDOM

No one complains when I buy junk food.
No one complains when I load the dishwasher wrong.
No one to ask before I make plans.
No one to scowl.
No one.

Oh my, I'm free.

ADVICE I

Music, my dear–
It will get you through.

i found that song–
taking my first breath,
and not breathing at all

i've never felt so seen

SPARKLE

It doesn't get easier, you just get stronger

I must be a diamond by now

postscript

GENERATIONS

My grandfather left my grandmother for their neighbour.
My father left my mother for online strangers.
My husband left me for a coworker.

Betrayed women, the entire lineage.

Praying for change,
Please God,
Let this end with me.

Gift my daughter with loyalty.

ADVICE II

Are you happy?
I start crying, nodding
Why are you crying?
I don't know, everything
Does he still give you a hard time?
I nod again, yes, no, I don't know
Life is too short you know
There's tears in her eyes
Because she knows pain too
And she knows how little time we have
You have to try and enjoy life while you can
I nod, I know

But I didn't actually know
Until I felt the sadness of time
Melt through her eyes and into mine.

THERAPY

    Hi.
Hi.
    Do you have anything you want to talk about today?
No.
    No?
I'm happy.
    You're happy?
I am.
    You've come a long way.
I know.
    It's nice to hear.
Thank you,
I feel like I can breathe again,
Like a comedown from an adrenaline rush,
Like I'm no longer in survival mode.
    You didn't realize you were in fight or flight?
No I didn't.
    And now?
It's calm, too calm.
I'm waiting for the ball to drop.
    What if there is no ball?
Is this normal life,
Contentment?
    Yes, that's the goal.
I think I'm here,
But I'm scared to lose it.
    Just enjoy it.
Enjoy it..
That's a novel concept.
    It is.
Okay I'll try.

ABOUT THE AUTHOR

S.M. Winter resides in Canada where she is happily remarried to a wonderful man. They are raising her daughter on a peaceful property surrounded by nature in a home filled with love.

These poems were an outlet of therapy while she navigated a tumultuous divorce through the second half of her twenties. Never intended for anyone's eyes, but courageously here they are.

If she can offer words to anyone in a similar situation it is: "Give yourself grace, and time. All the answers may not even be found in this lifetime, and that's okay."

She is currently working on her next collection; POEMS OF LOST.

www.smwinterpoetry.com

Coming soon:

POEMS OF LOST

preview

WICK

i can still see
the twinkle
in your eyes
playful smirk
dancing over the fish tacos between us
falling in love;
instantly
obsessively

a flame burning bright
cursed with a short wick

LUSH

one bottle of red
leads to two
always with you

cheeks flush
look in my eyes
i need to melt

that smile
come kiss me
while i'm tipsy

our problems
his and hers
but tonight
we have none

just kiss me
while i'm tipsy
we're fools

CHURCH

he held out his hands
begging for communion
catching the crude oil
that gurgled up my throat
spilling down my chin

good girl, let it out

Illustrations and cover art by the lovely
LC Wilson. IG: @sketchesforants

Special thanks to KM Flaherty for her editorial guidance.

www.smwinterpoetry.com

IG: smwinterpoetry

POEMS OF DIVORCE

POEMS OF DIVORCE
Copyright © 2024 by S.M. Winter.
All rights reserved.
ISBN 978-1-7383172-0-2

www.ingramcontent.com/pod-product-compliance
Lightning Source LLC
LaVergne TN
LVHW020116080426
835507LV00042B/1904